brownies

brownies
brownies

& blondies

blondies
blondies

brownies
brownies
brownies

& blondies
blondies
blondies

sam dixon

Seriously Delicious Recipes to Make at Home

Photography by Matthew Hague

Quadrille

Quadrille, Penguin Random House UK,
One Embassy Gardens, 8 Viaduct Gardens,
London SW11 7BW

Quadrille Publishing Limited is part of
the Penguin Random House group of
companies whose addresses can be found
at global.penguinrandomhouse.com

Penguin
Random House
UK

Published by Quadrille in 2025

www.penguin.co.uk

A CIP catalogue record for this book is
available from the British Library

ISBN 9781837833320
10 9 8 7 6 5 4 3 2 1

Colour reproduction by F1

Printed in China by C&C Offset Printing Co., Ltd.

The authorised representative in the EEA is
Penguin Random House Ireland, Morrison
Chambers, 32 Nassau Street, Dublin
D02 YH68.

Penguin Random House is committed
to a sustainable future for our business,
our readers and our planet. This book is
made from Forest Stewardship Council®
certified paper.

Managing Director
Sarah Lavelle

Commissioning Editor
Stacey Cleworth

Designer
Katy Everett

Photographer
Matthew Hague

Food Stylist
Sam Dixon

Food Stylist Assistants
Beatriz Moreno, Lucy Cottle

Prop Stylist
Max Robinson

Head of Production
Stephen Lang

Production Controller
Sumayyah Waheed

contents

introduction

Brownies and blondies are the classic household baking staple: the basis of many people's sweet treat repertoires. They have a lot of similarities, but are so different in flavour. You have your brownie, which is always made with cocoa powder and/or dark chocolate. It is dense and gooey in texture and, in my personal opinion, shouldn't be cakey, but each to their own! Blondies are buttery, mostly fudgy in texture and almost butterscotch-like in flavour from the brown sugar and vanilla. Both can have added ingredients that complement their base flavour, such as nuts, fruit or spices.

Among these recipes you have your classic brownie and blondie, plus versions that are adapted to be vegan or gluten-free, and more tips on how to substitute eggs and dairy. Plus, you'll find an exploration of various flavour combinations: anything from the popular cheesecake brownie and peanut butter blondie to not-so-traditional pandan and coconut or tahini and halva blondies. There is something for everyone here – it's your adventure!

Any ingredients that are hard to find in your local supermarket, such as pandan extract, kadayif or halva, can be bought fairly easily online on sites such as Amazon. Unless you have an Asian or Turkish/Middle Eastern supermarket at your disposal, where these ingredients are readily available.

These recipes are both doable and delicious, and will ensure you get perfect brownies and blondies every time. Great options for a midday sweet snack or a fancy dinner party dessert, and tips on how to prep ahead, or to store and keep fresh.

equipment & ingredients

Freestanding mixer or electric whisk:
these are pretty helpful if you want that crisp, almost meringue-like, surface on your brownie or blondie – but it's not necessary if you don't have either. They can all be made with a hand whisk and will be equally delicious.

baking tins
20cm (8in) and/or 23cm (9in) square baking tins are useful or can be similar in size; it doesn't have to be square – it could be rectangular, with roughly the same volume. For example, use a 20 x 30cm (8 x 12in) tin instead of a 23cm (9in) square one. Just make sure that the tin is 5cm (2in) deep.

chocolate
I always use dark chocolate with 70% cocoa solids in my brownies as it has a deeper flavour and is less sweet.

butter
I use unsalted butter for brownies and blondies as it's easier to control the amount of salt you add to your recipe by adding it separately.

gluten-free ingredients
If you want a gluten-free version, you can swap out the flour and baking powder for gluten-free plain flour and baking powder, no problem. Sometimes gluten-free flour makes your bakes even more fudgy.

vegan substitutions
To make a recipe vegan, swap out the butter for vegan butter and substitute the eggs with flaxseed soaked in water: to substitute one egg (scale up as necessary), mix 1 tablespoon of milled flaxseed with 3 tablespoons of cold water in a small bowl and leave to soak for 5 minutes. Or you could also substitute with apple purée (unsweetened apple sauce): use 63g (2¼oz) of apple purée for every egg required in the recipe. However, you will get a bit more flavour from the apple purée, so it's best used in any of the bakes that include fruit or spices. Another thing to note is that when using fruit purées, bakes tend to be a little denser, so it's best to add ¼ teaspoon of baking powder for every 63g (2¼oz) of fruit purée to lighten it.

tips

- All the batters can be frozen in the tin before baking and kept in the freezer for up to 6 months – that way you can make ahead and bake off as and when. Just make sure you defrost fully first.

- Baked brownies and blondies can be frozen for up to 6 months too, to keep them fresh. Otherwise, store them in an airtight container in a cool dry place for up to 5 days, or for up to 3 days in the fridge if there's fresh cream or cheesecake in them.

- With brownies and blondies, it's better to slightly underbake then overbake, so err on the side of caution and take them out sooner rather than later. Signs to look out for are a firm and crisp top and edges, and when you press gently on the top (careful of burning yourself!), there's still softness in the centre, but not so much that it's like raw cake batter. You can also insert a cocktail stick or knife – if there are still moist and sticky crumbs attached, then you're good to go, but if the stick or knife is totally wet with raw batter, the bake needs a little longer.

- Try really, really hard to let your bake cool in the tin before eating! I know, it's hard, I've been there too. But if you want a fudgy but firm consistency as opposed to a sloppy mess, patience is key!

brow

brow

brow

brow

ynies

triple choc brownies

Makes 9–16

This is the classic brownie, the OG. It is gooey with crisp edges and ever so slightly salty. If you prefer, you can omit the chocolate chunks, or you could even swap them out for walnut pieces. You do you. And if you're gluten free, you can swap the flour and baking powder for gluten-free options.

250g (9oz) unsalted butter
200g (7oz) dark chocolate (70% cocoa solids)
1 tsp flaky sea salt, plus extra for the top
200g (7oz) light brown soft sugar
100g (3½oz) caster (superfine) sugar
3 large eggs
1 tsp vanilla extract
70g (2½oz) plain (all-purpose) flour
50g (1¾oz) cocoa powder
½ tsp baking powder
100g (3½oz) milk chocolate chunks
100g (3½oz) white chocolate chunks

Preheat the oven to 160ºC fan (315ºF/gas 4) and grease and line a 23cm (9in) square baking tin with greaseproof paper.

In a large heatproof bowl set over a pan of just-simmering water (make sure the bottom of the bowl doesn't touch the water), melt the butter, dark chocolate and salt, stirring every now and then. Once melted and glossy, take off the heat and leave to cool slightly.

Whisk together the sugars, eggs and vanilla until pale and fluffy and almost doubled in size (this should take a couple of minutes).

In a separate bowl, whisk together the flour, cocoa powder and baking powder and set aside.

Slowly add the melted chocolate to the egg and sugar mixture and gently fold in until just combined. Then fold in the flour and cocoa powder mixture and the chocolate chunks, being careful not to overmix.

Pour this into the prepared tin, sprinkle with a large pinch of sea salt flakes and bake in the oven for 35–40 minutes. You want the top to be crisp and the centre to have a firm wobble.

Leave to cool in the tin for at least an hour before slicing up.

vegan classic brownies

vg

Makes 9–16

Everything you could possibly want in a brownie, but make it vegan. Flaxseed makes a very good egg substitute and the sugar syrup is what creates that glossy and meringue-like texture on the top. Feel free to swap out the chocolate chips/ walnuts for other fillings, such as raspberries, vegan fudge pieces, other types of nuts, dried fruit – whatever you fancy!

3 tbsp ground flaxseed

150g (5½oz) vegan dark chocolate
  (70% cocoa solids)

180g (6¼oz) vegan butter

Pinch of flaky sea salt, plus extra for the top

200g (7oz) light brown soft sugar

100g (3½oz) caster (superfine) sugar

150g (5½oz) plain (all-purpose) flour

50g (1¾oz) cocoa powder

½ tsp baking powder

1 tsp vanilla extract

150g (5½oz) vegan dark chocolate chips

100g (3½oz) chopped walnuts (optional)

Preheat the oven to 170ºC fan (325ºF/gas 5) and grease and line a 23cm (9in) square baking tin with greaseproof paper.

Activate the flaxseed by mixing it with 135ml (4½fl oz) water in a small bowl and set aside for 10 minutes.

Melt the chocolate, vegan butter and salt together in a large heatproof bowl set over a pan of just-simmering water (make sure the bottom of the bowl doesn't touch the water), whisking until glossy.

In a saucepan, heat the sugars together with 100ml (3½fl oz) water until the sugar has completely dissolved.

Whisk together the flour, cocoa powder and baking powder in a separate bowl.

Whisk the sugar syrup into the melted chocolate, then add the flaxseed and vanilla. Fold in the flour mixture carefully, then add the chocolate chips and walnuts, if using.

Pour the batter into the prepared tin and smooth the top even. Sprinkle with a little more flaky sea salt and bake for 25–30 minutes until the top is crisp but the centre is still a little soft.

Leave to cool completely in the tin before slicing up.

flourless almond and sour cherry brownies

gf

Makes 9

Flourless, so gluten-free, these brownies are enriched with ground almonds that provide a delicious nutty texture, without kimping on the gooey-ness, and are studded with tart sour cherries to offset the richness.

200g (7oz) unsalted butter
200g (7oz) dark chocolate (at least 70% cocoa
    solids), broken up into small pieces
2 large eggs
200g (7oz) light brown soft sugar
1 tsp vanilla extract
½ tsp salt
200g (7oz) ground almonds
100g (3½oz) dark chocolate chips
100g (3½oz) dried sour cherries

Preheat the oven to 160ºC fan (315ºF/gas 4) and grease and line a 20cm (8in) square baking tin with greaseproof paper.

First, in a large heatproof bowl set over a saucepan of barely simmering water (make sure the bottom of the bowl doesn't touch the water), melt the butter and chocolate together gently, stirring every now and then. Once melted, leave to cool slightly.

In a separate large bowl, whisk together the eggs, sugar, vanilla and salt until pale and doubled in size – it's best to use a freestanding mixer or electric whisk here, if you have one.

Slowly pour in the melted chocolate mixture and fold in gently, along with the ground almonds, chocolate chips and sour cherries until just combined – you don't want to overmix.

Pour the batter into the prepared tin and bake for 30–35 minutes until the top is crisp but it's still gooey in the middle.

Leave to cool in the tin before slicing up.

marbled cheesecake brownies

Makes 12

Dark chocolate fudgy brownie marbled with soft, creamy vanilla cheesecake – two great desserts rolled into one.

For the brownie

150g (5½oz) unsalted butter

150g (5½oz) dark chocolate (at least 70% cocoa solids)

Pinch of salt

2 large eggs

200g (7oz) caster (superfine) sugar

½ tsp vanilla extract

60g (2¼oz) plain (all-purpose) flour

½ tsp baking powder

30g (1oz) cocoa powder

For the cheesecake

280g (10oz) cream cheese

60g (2¼oz) caster (superfine) sugar

1 egg

1 tsp vanilla extract

First, make the brownie. Preheat the oven to 170°C fan (325°F/gas 5) and grease and line a deep 20 x 30cm (8 x 12in) baking tray with greaseproof paper.

Melt the butter and chocolate with the salt in a large heatproof bowl set over a pan of barely simmering water (make sure the bottom of the bowl doesn't touch the water) until melted and glossy.

In a separate large bowl, whisk together the eggs, sugar and vanilla until pale, fluffy and doubled in size – this is best done with an electric whisk or in a freestanding mixer, if you have one.

Carefully fold the melted chocolate mixture into the eggs and sugar.

Whisk together the flour, baking powder and cocoa powder in a separate bowl, then fold this carefully into the brownie batter. Pour this into

the prepared tin, leaving about a fifth of the batter in the bowl – this is for swirling. Smooth the brownie batter out.

Now start the cheesecake mixture. In a large bowl, whisk together the cream cheese and sugar, then add the egg and vanilla and mix until smooth.

Pour the cheesecake mixture carefully over the brownie batter, then dot blobs of the reserved batter over the top. With a knife, swirl and marble the mixtures together in a random pattern.

Bake for 30 minutes, until the edges are crisp, the cheesecake is lightly golden brown and an inserted knife comes out with a few moist crumbs.

Leave to cool completely in the tin, then refrigerate for at least 1 hour before slicing and serving.

tiramisu
brownies

Makes 12

Why not chuck a brownie in with a tiramisu? Why. Not.
The coffee in the brownie base really brings out the dark
chocolate richness, and it's topped with coffee-soaked sponge
fingers and not-too-sweet vanilla-spiked mascarpone cream
– you'll be eating this straight out of the tray with a spoon.

For the coffee brownie

150g (5½oz) dark chocolate (at least
   70% cocoa solids)
150g (5½oz) unsalted butter
Pinch of salt
60ml (2fl oz) strong coffee (brewed or instant)
2 large eggs
100g (3½oz) caster (superfine) sugar
100g (3½oz) light brown soft sugar
½ tsp vanilla extract
60g (2¼oz) plain (all-purpose) flour
40g (1½oz) cocoa powder
½ tsp baking powder

For the tiramisu top

400ml (14fl oz) strong coffee (brewed
   or instant), cooled
24–30 sponge fingers (savoiardi)
300g (10½oz) double (heavy) cream
50g (1¾oz) caster (superfine) sugar
2 tsp vanilla bean paste
300g (10½oz) mascarpone cheese
Unsweetened cocoa powder, for dusting

Preheat the oven to 160ºC fan (315ºF/gas 4) and grease and line a deep 20 x 30cm (8 x 12in) baking tray with greaseproof paper.

Make the brownies first by melting the chocolate and butter with the salt and coffee in a heatproof bowl over a pan of barely simmering water (make sure the bottom of the bowl doesn't touch the water), then set aside to cool slightly.

Whisk together the eggs, sugars and vanilla until pale, fluffy and doubled in size – this is best done with an electric whisk or in a freestanding mixer, if you have one.

Gently fold in the melted chocolate, then sift over the flour, cocoa powder and baking powder and fold this in until just combined, being careful not to overmix.

Pour the batter into the prepared tin and bake for 20–25 minutes until crisp round the edges and just set in the middle. Leave to cool in the tin completely before adding the toppings.

Once the brownie is cool, pour the strong coffee into a wide, shallow bowl. One by one, dip the sponge fingers into the coffee until nicely coated and slightly soaked – not too soaked though as you don't want them to be too mushy – then arrange them on the surface of the brownie until it's completely covered in a single layer of fingers.

In a large bowl, whip the cream, caster sugar and vanilla until soft peaks form, then whisk in the mascarpone briefly – you don't want to overmix and make it too stiff.

Dollop the cream over the sponge fingers and smooth the top, then give it a nice dusting of cocoa powder.

Refrigerate for 2 hours, or overnight. Slice up or spoon out when ready to serve.

hazelnut praline brownies

Makes 9

You can use whatever nuts you like here, or a combination. I just love hazelnuts with chocolate, and the crunchy caramel shards add another texture.

For the hazelnut praline
100g (3½oz) hazelnuts, toasted
200g (7oz) caster (superfine) sugar
Pinch of salt

For the brownie
200g (7oz) unsalted butter
200g (7oz) dark chocolate (70% cocoa solids)
Pinch of salt
3 eggs
170g (6oz) light brown sugar
1 tsp vanilla extract
70g (2½oz) plain (all-purpose) flour
40g (1½oz) cocoa powder
1 tsp baking powder

Preheat the oven to 160ºC fan (315ºF/gas 4) and grease and line a 20cm (8in) square baking tin with greaseproof paper.

Lay out the toasted hazelnuts on a baking tray lined with greaseproof paper.

In a small heavy-based pan, heat the sugar with 2 tablespoons of water on a low–medium heat to dissolve the sugar, before increasing to medium–high heat to caramelize it – keep a close eye on it. You want to catch it just before it goes too dark; you can tell by smell and sight. Once the caramel is a deep golden brown colour, take the pan off the heat and pour the caramel carefully over the hazelnuts, then sprinkle with the pinch of salt. Leave to cool and harden while you get on with your brownie.

Melt the butter and chocolate with the salt in a heatproof bowl set over a pan of barely simmering water (make sure the bottom of the bowl doesn't touch the water) until glossy and combined.

Whisk together the eggs, sugar and vanilla until pale and doubled in size – this is best done with an electric whisk or in a freestanding mixer, if you have one.

Roughly chop the praline and set half aside. Put the other half in a heavy-duty blender and blitz to an almost nut-butter consistency. (If you don't have a blender, chop that half really fine by hand – it'll be just as delicious.)

Carefully fold the melted chocolate and butter into the egg mixture, then sift the flour, cocoa powder and baking powder over the batter and fold this gently in too.

Fold in some of the roughly chopped hazelnut praline (reserving some for scattering over the top), then pour the batter into the prepared tray.

Smooth the brownie level before breaking up chunks of the praline 'nut butter' and scattering this over. Scatter over the reserved roughly chopped praline and bake for 30–35 minutes or until the top of the brownie is crisp but there's still a very slight wobble.

Leave to cool completely before slicing up and serving.

mint choc chip brownies

Makes 9–16

Mint and chocolate is not for everyone; however, mint chocolate lightens up a rich and gooey brownie with a freshness that makes these dangerously easy to eat too many of.

175g (6oz) unsalted butter
100g (3½oz) dark chocolate
1 tsp salt
3 large eggs
150g (5½oz) light brown soft sugar
150g (5½oz) caster (superfine) sugar
1 tbsp peppermint extract
70g (2½oz) plain (all-purpose) flour
40g (1½oz) cocoa powder
½ tsp baking powder
150g (5½oz) mint chocolate, coarsely chopped
   (whatever kind you fancy, dark or milk)

Preheat the oven to 160ºC fan (315ºF/gas 4) and grease and line a 23cm (9in) square baking tin with greaseproof paper.

Melt the butter, dark chocolate and salt together in a heatproof bowl set over a pan of barely simmering water (make sure the bottom of the bowl doesn't touch the water), then set aside to cool slightly.

Whisk the eggs, sugars and peppermint extract until pale and fluffy and doubled in size – this is best done with an electric whisk or in a freestanding mixer, if you have one, and should take at least 5 minutes.

Carefully fold in the melted chocolate mixture, then sift the flour, cocoa powder and baking powder over and fold this in, adding the mint chocolate chunks halfway.

Pour the batter into the prepared tin and bake for 30–35 minutes until the top and sides are crisp and the middle is firm but slightly gooey.

Leave to cool in the tin completely before slicing up.

pistachio and rose water brownies

Makes 9–16

A very luxurious brownie, whose floral notes of rose water paired with sweet, earthy, nutty pistachios transports you to a different continent.

For the pistachio frangipane
60g (2¼oz) pistachios
60g (2¼oz) butter, softened
60g (2¼oz) caster (superfine) sugar
1 egg white
Pinch of salt

For the brownie
185g (6½oz) unsalted butter
185g (6½oz) dark chocolate (70% cocoa solids)
Pinch of salt
3 eggs
200g (7oz) light brown soft sugar
3 tbsp rose water

80g (2¾oz) plain (all-purpose) flour
40g (1½oz) cocoa powder
½ tsp baking powder

For topping (optional)
2 heaped tbsp icing (confectioners') sugar
1 tsp rose water
1 heaped tbsp pistachios, roughly chopped
Edible rose petals, for decorating (optional)

Preheat the oven to 170ºC fan (325ºF/gas 5) and grease and line a 23cm (9in) square baking tin with greaseproof paper.

To make the pistachio frangipane, blitz up the pistachios in a food processor until you have fine crumbs – don't over process or they will turn into butter.

Next, add the softened butter to the food processor with the pistachios, then add the sugar, egg white and salt. Blitz until you get a creamy frangipane, then set this aside while you make your brownie.

Melt the butter and chocolate with the salt in a heatproof bowl set over a pan of barely simmering water (make sure the bottom of the bowl doesn't touch the water) until glossy and melted, then take off the heat.

Whisk together the eggs, sugar and rose water until thick and pale – this is best done with an electric whisk or in a freestanding mixer, if you have one. Then gently fold in the melted chocolate mixture.

Sift over the flour, cocoa powder and baking powder and fold this into the brownie mixture until just combined.

Pour the batter into the prepared tin and smooth level. Dollop spoonfuls of the pistachio frangipane over the surface of the batter and, with a knife, swirl it carefully through so the top has a marbled effect.

Bake for 30–40 minutes until the frangipane is golden brown and the brownie is crisp but gooey in the middle. Leave to cool completely in the tin.

Make a glaze by mixing the icing sugar with the rose water and enough water to make an opaque but runny icing. Drizzle the icing over the brownie and decorate with the chopped pistachios and the edible rose petals, if you're feeling extra fancy. Let the icing set before slicing up.

candied orange and fennel seed brownies

Makes 9–16

Slightly more demure than a Terry's Chocolate Orange, with fennel seeds to add a more grown-up aniseed flavour, and pieces of candied peel for texture.

200g (7oz) unsalted butter
200g (7oz) dark chocolate (at least
    70% cocoa solids)
½ tsp salt
1 tbsp fennel seeds
3 eggs
200g (7oz) light brown soft sugar
Finely grated zest of 2 oranges
80g (2¾oz) plain (all-purpose) flour
½ tsp baking powder
100g (3½oz) candied orange peel
150g (5½oz) dark orange chocolate,
    broken up into chunks

Preheat the oven to 160ºC fan (315ºF/gas 4) and grease and line a 23cm (9in) square baking tin with greaseproof paper.

Melt the butter and chocolate with the salt and fennel seeds in a heatproof bowl set over a pan of barely simmering water (make sure the bottom of the bowl doesn't touch the water) until glossy and melted, then take off the heat and set aside to cool slightly.

Whisk together the eggs and sugar until thick and pale and doubled in size – this is best done with an electric whisk or in a freestanding mixer, if you have one. Then gently fold in the melted chocolate mixture, followed by the orange zest.

Sift the flour and baking powder over the batter and fold in carefully.

Pour the batter into the prepared tin and scatter over the candied orange peel and dark orange chocolate chunks so that the pieces are evenly distributed.

Bake for 30–35 minutes until the top is shiny and crisp and the centre is firm but still a little gooey.

Leave to cool completely in the tin before slicing and serving.

skillet chocolate chestnut brownie pudding

Serves 8

A delectable chocolate pudding, similar to a fondant, but a great big one and with a slight nutty, chewy texture from the chestnuts. So good with cold pouring cream or ice cream.

100g (3½oz) unsalted butter
100g (3½oz) dark chocolate
2 eggs and 2 egg yolks
150g (5½oz) light brown soft sugar
200g (7oz) chestnut purée
1 tbsp vanilla extract
70g (2½oz) plain (all-purpose) flour
30g (1oz) cocoa powder, plus extra for dusting
½ tsp salt
Double (heavy) cream or ice cream, to serve

Butter a 23cm (9in) skillet or similar-sized oven-proof pudding dish, make sure it fits in a larger deep ovenproof dish and preheat the oven to 160ºC (315ºF) fan, gas 4.

Melt the butter and chocolate in a heatproof bowl set over a pan of barely simmering water (make sure the bottom of the bowl doesn't touch the water) until glossy and melted, then take off the heat and set aside to cool slightly.

Whisk the eggs, egg yolks and sugar into the melted chocolate, then add the chestnut purée and vanilla.

Sift the flour, cocoa powder and salt over the batter and fold in until just combined – you don't want to overmix!

Pour the batter into the prepared skillet and bake for 12–16 minutes – you want it to be fairly gooey in the centre (more so than a normal brownie) but crisp on the top.

Dust with cocoa powder and serve warm with cold cream or ice cream.

malted milk brownie ice cream sando

Makes 9–16

My personal favourite dessert to whip out at a BBQ or dinner party, it's easy to make ahead and the homemade no-churn ice cream always impresses.

For the brownie

150g (5½oz) unsalted butter
150g (5½oz) dark chocolate (at least 70% cocoa solids)
Pinch of salt
2 large eggs
200g (7oz) caster (superfine) sugar
½ tsp vanilla extract
60g (2¼oz) plain (all-purpose) flour
30g (1oz) Ovaltine powder
½ tsp baking powder
100g (3½oz) dark chocolate chips

For the malted milk ice cream

400g (14oz) double (heavy) cream
200g (7oz) condensed milk
4 heaped tbsp Ovaltine powder

Preheat the oven to 160ºC fan (315ºF/gas 4) and grease and line two 23cm (9in) square baking tins with greaseproof paper – if you don't have two tins, just cook the layers one at a time.

Melt the butter and chocolate with the salt in a heatproof bowl set over a pan of barely simmering water (make sure the bottom of the bowl doesn't touch the water) until glossy and melted, then take off the heat and set aside to cool slightly.

Whisk the eggs, sugar and vanilla together until frothy, then slowly pour in the melted chocolate, whisking as you go until mixed.

In a separate bowl, whisk together the flour, Ovaltine and baking powder, then fold this through the batter, adding the chocolate chips halfway through folding.

Split the batter between the two trays (or just add half the batter to a tray if you have only one) and spread evenly. Bake for 20 minutes or until firm to the touch and crisp on top.

Leave the layer(s) to cool completely in the tins. Once cool, remove one brownie from the tin and leave the second layer in the tin.

To make the ice cream, whip the double cream with an electric whisk or in a freestanding mixer until stiff-ish peaks form, then fold in the condensed milk and Ovaltine carefully until combined. Pour this over the brownie that you have left in the tin, then sandwich the ice cream with the other brownie. Clingfilm (plastic wrap) the tray and put it in the freezer for at least 5 hours, or overnight.

When you're ready to serve, take the sando out the freezer and let it sit for 10 minutes before slicing up into 9 or 16 even pieces and serving immediately. If you only want one or two at a time, cut and wrap all the pieces individually, then pop the rest back in the freezer and you'll have ready-made ice-cream sandos whenever you fancy!

mochi
brownies
gf

Makes 9–16

A texturally different take on a classic brownie, all chocolate fudginess but with a slightly bouncy chewiness. Made with glutinous rice flour, this is also gluten free.

80g (2¾oz) unsalted butter
200g (7oz) dark chocolate (70% cocoa solids)
200g (7oz) glutinous rice flour/mochiko flour
60g (2¼oz) cocoa powder
200g (7oz) caster (superfine) sugar
100g (3½oz) light brown sugar
1 tsp flaky salt, plus extra for sprinkling
2 tsp gluten-free baking powder
400ml (14fl oz) whole milk
2 eggs
1 tsp vanilla extract
100g (3½oz) dark chocolate chips

Preheat the oven to 160ºC fan (315ºF/gas 4) and grease and line a 23cm (9in) square baking tin with greaseproof paper.

Melt the butter and chocolate in a heatproof bowl set over a pan of barely simmering water (make sure the bottom of the bowl doesn't touch the water) until glossy and melted, then take off the heat and set aside to cool slightly.

In a food processor, blitz together the flour, cocoa powder, sugars, salt and baking powder until blended.

Add the melted chocolate mixture, milk, eggs and vanilla and blitz until completely combined.

Pour the batter into the prepared tin, sprinkle over the chcocolate chips and extra salt and bake for 20–25 minutes until the brownie is firm to the touch.

Leave to cool completely in the tin before slicing up.

chocolate mousse brownies

Makes 9–16

This is a truly indulgent dessert: a rich chocolate brownie base with a thick layer of light airy chocolate mousse. An elite brownie to be eaten off a plate with a fork while sitting at the table, rather than by hand standing up over a kitchen counter.

For the brownie base
125g (4½oz) unsalted butter
100g (3½oz) dark chocolate (70% cocoa solids)
Pinch of salt
1 egg
150g (5½oz) light brown muscovado sugar
½ tsp vanilla extract
40g (1½oz) plain (all-purpose) flour
20g (¾oz) cocoa powder
¼ tsp baking powder

For the milk choc mousse top
225g (8oz) dark chocolate
½ tsp flaky salt, plus more for sprinkling
6 large eggs, separated
4 tbsp caster (superfine) sugar
225g (8oz) double (heavy) cream

First make the brownie. Preheat the oven to 170ºC fan (325ºF/gas 5) and grease and line a 23cm (9in) square baking tin with greaseproof paper.

Melt the butter and chocolate with the salt in a heatproof bowl set over a pan of barely simmering water (make sure the bottom of the bowl doesn't touch the water) until glossy and melted.

Whisk together the egg, sugar and vanilla until frothy – this is best done with an electric whisk or in a freestanding mixer, if you have one. Slowly pour in the melted chocolate mixture, whisking continuously as you add it.

Sift the flour, cocoa and baking powder over the batter and fold this in gently until just combined.

Pour the batter into the prepared tin and smooth level. Bake for 20 minutes until firm to the touch, then leave to cool completely in the tin.

Once the brownie has cooled, start making the mousse. Melt the chocolate with the salt in a heatproof bowl over a pan of simmering water, then set aside to cool.

Whisk the egg whites with an electric whisk or in a freestanding mixer until soft peaks form, then slowly add the sugar and continue whisking until you have stiff glossy peaks.

In a separate bowl, whisk the double cream to soft peaks.

Whisk the egg yolks into the melted chocolate, then fold in the whipped cream. Finally, gently fold in the egg whites, in three batches, being careful not to knock the air out.

Once all the egg whites are folded in, pour the chocolate mousse over the cooled chocolate brownie and smooth over carefully.

Pop the tray into the fridge for at least 4 hours, or overnight, for the mousse to set. Sprinkle with a little flaky sea salt before slicing up (or spooning up) and serving.

black forest brownies

Makes 9–16

A retro classic: cream, chocolate and cherries – some things from the past are definitely good enough to keep bringing back.

brownies

200g (7oz) unsalted butter
200g (7oz) dark chocolate (at least
   70% cocoa solids)
½ tsp salt
3 eggs
150g (5½oz) light brown soft sugar
100g (3½oz) caster (superfine) sugar
2 tbsp kirsch (optional)
80g (2¾oz) plain (all-purpose) flour
40g (1½oz) cocoa powder
½ tsp baking powder
200g (7oz) fresh or frozen cherries
100g (3½oz) cherry jam

For the decoration
200g (7oz) double (heavy) cream
9–16 glacé cherries
Dark chocolate shavings

Preheat the oven to 160ºC fan (315ºF/gas 4) and grease and line a 23cm (9in) square baking tin with greaseproof paper.

Melt the butter and chocolate with the salt in a heatproof bowl set over a pan of barely simmering water (make sure the bottom of the bowl doesn't touch the water) until glossy and melted.

Whisk together the eggs, sugars and kirsch, if using, until thick, pale and doubled in size – this is best done with an electric whisk or in a freestanding mixer, if you have one. Then, lightly fold in the melted chocolate mixture.

Sift the flour, cocoa powder and baking powder over the batter and gently fold this in. Pour the batter into the prepared tin, then scatter over the cherries. Dollop spoonfuls of the cherry jam over the surface of the batter and, with a knife, swirl it carefully through so the top has a marbled effect.

Bake for 30–35 minutes until the surface is shiny and crispy and the centre is just firm with a slight wobble.

While you're letting the brownie cool in the tin, whip the double cream to soft peaks.

Slice up the brownie into squares and dollop a tablespoon of cream on the top of each slice. Top with a glacé cherry and dark chocolate shavings.

cornflake crispy brownie

Makes 9–16

I am extremely partial to a cornflake crispy cake, so I stuck one on a brownie. You have the soft chocolatey brownie base and crunchy, crispy cornflake topping for a textural sensation; it's two sweet treats rolled into one.

For the brownie base
150g (5½oz) unsalted butter
150g (5½oz) dark chocolate (at least
   70% cocoa solids), chopped
Pinch of salt
2 large eggs
200g (7oz) caster (superfine) sugar
½ tsp vanilla extract
60g (2¼oz) plain (all-purpose) flour
30g (1oz) cocoa powder
½ tsp baking powder

For the cornflake crispy top
220g (7¾oz) dark or milk chocolate, chopped
80g (2¾oz) butter
3 tbsp golden syrup (light corn syrup)
Pinch of salt
100g (3½oz) cornflakes

Preheat the oven to 170ºC fan (325ºF/gas 5) and grease and line a 23cm (9in) square baking tin with greaseproof paper.

Make the brownie base first. Melt the butter and chocolate with the salt in a heatproof bowl set over a pan of barely simmering water (make sure the bottom of the bowl doesn't touch the water) until glossy and melted, then remove from the heat.

Once the chocolate mixture has cooled slightly, whisk in the eggs, sugar and vanilla.

Sift the flour, cocoa and baking powder over the batter and fold in carefully until just combined.

Pour the batter into the prepared tin and bake for 20–25 minutes, until it's firm to the touch. Leave to cool completely while you get on with the cornflake crispy top.

Melt the dark or milk chocolate in a large heatproof bowl with the butter, golden syrup and salt. Once melted, stir through the cornflakes, making sure they're completely covered in the chocolate. Spread this over the brownie base and smooth level as much as you can without pressing down too much.

Pop the brownie in the fridge for about 1 hour or more to set the cornflakes before cutting up and serving.

blon

blon

blon

blon

dies

dies

dies

dies

classic blondies

Makes 9

The classic blondie is buttery, almost caramelized in flavour from the brown sugar, ever so slightly salty, and studded with milk chocolate. You can swap out the plain flour for a gluten-free alternative to make this completely gluten free.

2 eggs
250g (9oz) light brown sugar
1½ tsp vanilla extract
200g (7oz) butter, melted
220g (7¾oz) plain (all-purpose) flour
   (or gluten-free flour)
1 tsp fine sea salt
200g (7oz) milk chocolate, chopped into chunks

Preheat the oven to 170ºC fan (325ºF/gas 5) and grease and line a 23cm (9in) square baking tin with greaseproof paper.

Whisk together the eggs, sugar and vanilla until pale and fluffy – this is best done with an electric whisk or in a freestanding mixer, if you have one. Slowly add the melted butter, whisking slowly as you go.

In a separate bowl, whisk together the flour and salt, then fold this carefully into the blondie mixture, along with the milk chocolate chunks, until just combined.

Pour the batter into the prepared tin and bake for 25–30 minutes until the surface is golden brown and crisp and the middle is slightly gooey.

Leave to cool completely in the tin before slicing up and serving.

apple and cinnamon swirl blondies

vg

Makes 9–16

Apple purée makes for a great egg substitute, but it does taste like apple – unlike flaxseed, which doesn't have much of a flavour – so it complements the cinnamon and fresh apple flavours.

For the blondie base
250g (9oz) vegan butter, melted
200g (7oz) light brown sugar
125g (4½oz) apple purée (unsweetened apple sauce)
1 apple, cored and grated
1 tsp vanilla extract
240g (8½oz) plain (all-purpose) flour
½ tsp baking powder
½ tsp salt

For the cinnamon sugar
60g (2¼oz) caster (superfine) sugar
1 tbsp ground cinnamon

Preheat the oven to 160ºC fan (315ºF/gas 4) and grease and line a 23cm (9in) square baking tin with greaseproof paper.

Whisk the melted vegan butter, brown sugar and apple purée together in a large bowl, then whisk in the grated apple and vanilla.

Sift the flour, baking powder and salt over the batter and fold in, then pour the batter into the prepared tin.

In a separate small bowl, mix together the caster sugar and cinnamon. Spoon this over the apple blondie mixture and swirl it into the batter slightly.

Bake for 25–30 minutes, until the top is crisp but it is still slightly soft in the centre.

Leave to cool completely in the tin before slicing up.

tahini, halva and dark choc blondies

Makes 9

Halva is a traditional Middle Eastern sweet, similar to fudge but more crumbly, which is usually made with a seed or nut-butter base. Crumbled over a buttery blondie and swirled with creamy, nutty tahini and crisp sesame seeds, it gives these blondies a delicious depth of flavour and texture.

200g (7oz) unsalted butter
180g (6¼oz) plain (all-purpose) flour
½ tsp salt
½ tsp baking powder
250g (9oz) light brown soft sugar
2 large eggs
2 tsp vanilla extract
100g (3½oz) halva, broken up
150g (5½oz) dark chocolate, roughly
   chopped into chunks
50g (1¾oz) runny tahini
2 tbsp sesame seeds, for sprinkling on top
   (can be a mixture of black and white or
   just one type)

Preheat the oven to 160ºC fan (315ºF/gas 4) and grease and line a 20cm (8in) square baking tin with greaseproof paper.

First make the brown butter by melting the butter gently in a small saucepan. Once melted, turn up the heat to medium and cook until the butter turns golden brown and you can see tiny specks of brown at the bottom of the pan, and it starts to smell nutty. This usually takes a few minutes; whisk occasionally so that it doesn't catch on the bottom of the pan and keep a close eye on it so that you don't burn it! Set aside to cool slightly.

In a bowl, whisk together the flour, salt and baking powder and set aside.

Pour the browned butter into a large separate bowl and whisk in the sugar, then add the eggs and vanilla and whisk until frothy.

Gently fold in the flour until just combined, then add the halva and chocolate chunks.

Pour the batter into your prepared tin. Now, with a teaspoon, drizzle over the tahini to make a pattern on the top of the blondie, then scatter over your sesame seeds. Bake for 25–30 minutes until the edges are crisp and the centre is just set.

Leave to cool in the tin before slicing up.

raspberry, white chocolate and cardamom blondies

Makes 12

The cardamom spice and tart raspberries balance out the sweetness of the white chocolate in this flavourful combination.

2 eggs
300g (10½oz) light brown sugar
2 tsp vanilla extract
250g (9oz) unsalted butter, melted
250g (9oz) plain (all-purpose) flour
1 tsp fine sea salt
½ tsp baking powder
2 tsp ground cardamom
200g (7oz) fresh or frozen raspberries
150g (5½oz) white chocolate, chopped
    into chunks

Preheat the oven to 170ºC fan (325ºF/gas 5) and grease and line a 20 x 30cm (8 x 12in) baking tin with greaseproof paper.

In a large bowl, whisk together the eggs, sugar and vanilla until pale and fluffy – this is best done with an electric whisk or in a freestanding mixer, if you have one. While still whisking, slowly pour in the melted butter.

In a separate bowl, whisk together the flour, salt, baking powder and cardamom. Fold this through the egg and butter mixture until just combined, then gently fold in two thirds of the raspberries and two-thirds of the white chocolate.

Pour the batter into the prepared tin, smooth level and top with the remaining raspberries and white chocolate.

Bake in the oven for 25–30 minutes until the blondie is crisp and shiny on top and an inserted knife comes out clean-ish – you want it to be a little gooey.

Leave to cool completely in the tin before cutting up and serving.

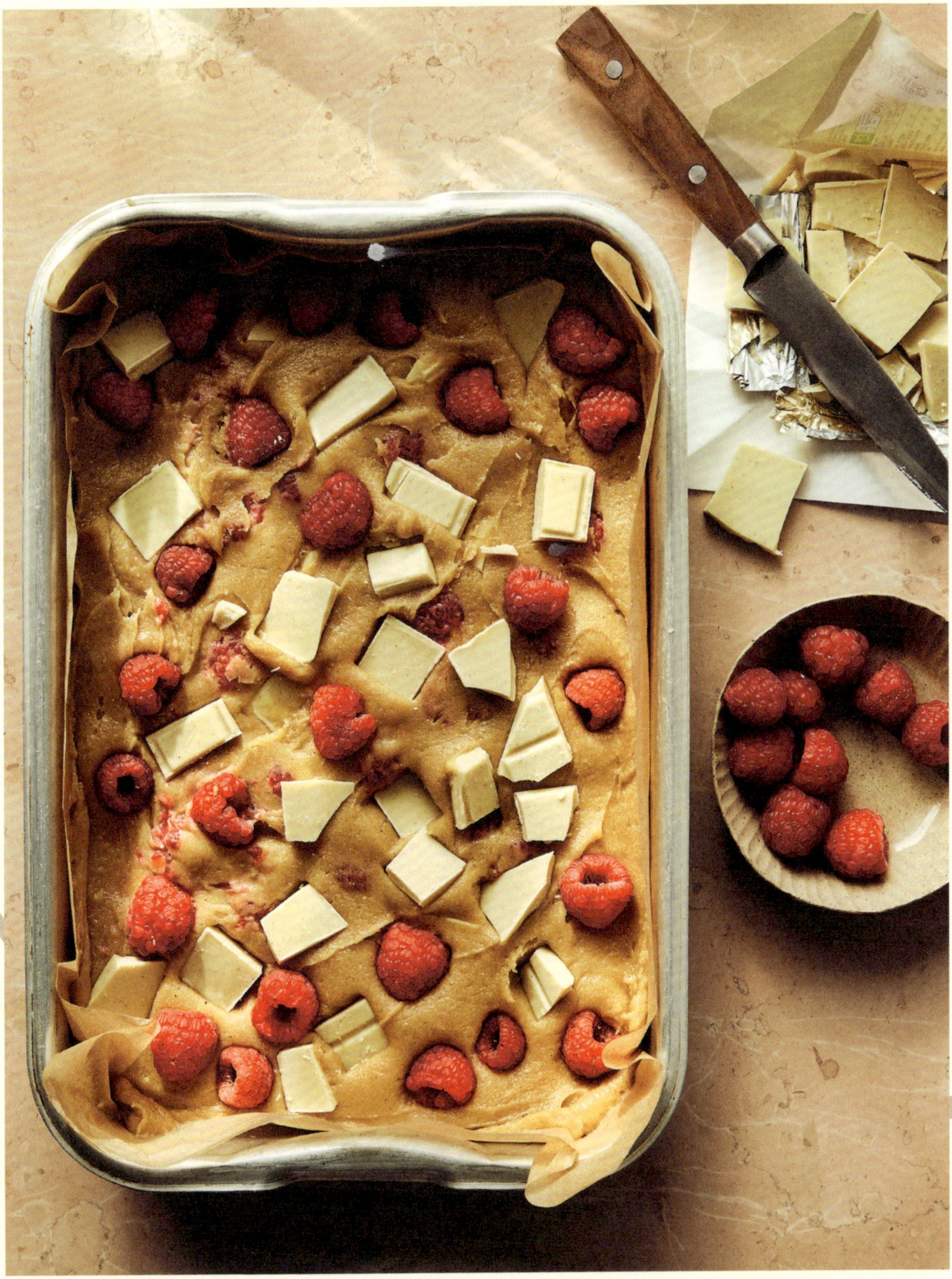

miso caramel and milk chocolate blondies

Makes 9–16

Sweet but umami miso caramel and milk chocolate works so well together. If you've only had miso in soup form or in savoury food, trust me – it adds another element of flavour to an already action-packed salted caramel.

2 eggs
250g (9oz) light brown sugar
1 tsp vanilla extract
175g (6oz) butter, melted
200g (7oz) plain (all-purpose) flour
¼ tsp baking powder
1 tsp salt
150g (5½oz) milk chocolate chunks
Ice cream, to serve

For the miso caramel
50g (1¾oz) light brown sugar
50g (1¾oz) caster (superfine) sugar
75g (2½oz) double (heavy) cream
25g (1oz) butter, chilled and cubed
Pinch of salt
½ tbsp white miso paste
½ tbsp lemon juice

Make the miso caramel by adding both sugars to a heavy-based saucepan with 1 tablespoon water. Put on a low–medium heat at first, and swirl the pan carefully so that the sugar melts evenly and slowly, to avoid crystallization – you don't want to stir it.

Once the sugars have melted, increase the heat to medium–high and let it bubble until caramelized and dark brown (make sure you catch it before it burns), then take off the heat.

Whisk in the cream – be careful, it'll spit! – then whisk in the butter, salt and miso paste. Once the butter has been completely emulsified, whisk in the lemon juice and leave it to one side to cool.

Preheat the oven to 160ºC fan (315ºF/gas 4) and grease and line a 23cm (9in) square baking tin with greaseproof paper.

Whisk together the eggs, sugar and vanilla until pale and fluffy, then whisk in the melted butter.

In a separate bowl, combine the flour, baking powder and salt, then fold this into the eggs and sugar.

Pour the batter into the prepared tin and smooth level, before scattering over the chocolate chunks, then spoon over three quarters of the miso caramel, swirling it into the batter slightly so it's evenly distributed.

Bake for 35–40 minutes until crisp and golden brown round the edges and still a little gooey in the centre.

Serve the blondies warm with ice cream, drizzled with the remaining miso caramel.

pandan and coconut blondies

Makes 9–16

Pandan is a leaf used in Asian cookery, especially in sweets, and its extract tastes like coconut and vanilla rolled into one – and it colours everything a lovely green hue. Paired with coconut and the caramel flavour of brown sugar, it's the perfect accompaniment to a blondie base.

2 large eggs

100g (3½oz) light brown sugar

150g (5½oz) caster (superfine) sugar

200g (7oz) unsalted butter, melted

1 tbsp pandan extract (the bright green one!)

180g (6¼oz) plain (all-purpose) flour

½ tsp salt

100g (3½oz) desiccated (dried shredded)
coconut

50g (1¾oz) flaked coconut (you want
large pieces)

Preheat the oven to 160ºC fan (315ºF/gas 4) and grease and line a 23cm (9in) square baking tin with greaseproof paper.

In a large bowl, whisk together the eggs and sugars until frothy, then slowly whisk in the melted butter and pandan extract.

Whisk together the flour, salt and desiccated coconut in a separate bowl, then gently fold this into the butter mixture until just combined and smooth – you don't want to overmix.

Pour the batter into the prepared tin and sprinkle over the coconut flakes. Bake for 25–30 minutes, until the edges are crisp and golden brown and the middle is just set.

Leave to cool in the tin before slicing up.

spiced pumpkin and pecan blondies

Makes 12

Think autumnal vibes; think two favourite American pie flavours rolled into one, but in a fudgy blondie bar.

150g (5½oz) pecans
250g (9oz) unsalted butter
2 eggs
300g (10½oz) light brown sugar
200g (7oz) pumpkin purée (from a tin is fine)
160g (5¾oz) plain (all-purpose) flour
½ tsp baking powder
1 tsp salt
1 tbsp ground cinnamon, plus extra to serve
½ tsp ground ginger
¼ tsp ground cloves
¼ tsp grated nutmeg
Softly whipped cream, to serve

Preheat the oven to 160ºC fan (315ºF/gas 4) and grease and line a 20 x 30cm (8 x 12in) baking tin with greaseproof paper.

Add the pecans to the tray and roast in the oven for about 15 minutes until toasted and golden brown. Set aside to cool before roughly chopping them.

Make the brown butter by melting the butter gently in a small saucepan. Once melted, turn up the heat to medium and cook until the butter turns golden brown and you can see tiny specks of brown at the bottom of the pan, and it starts to smell nutty. This usually takes a few minutes; whisk occasionally so that it doesn't catch on the bottom of the pan and keep a close eye on it so that you don't burn it! Set aside to cool slightly.

Whisk together the eggs and sugar until frothy, then whisk in the cooled brown butter and the pumpkin purée.

In a separate bowl, mix together the flour, baking powder, salt and spices, then fold this into the wet ingredients, adding the chopped pecans halfway.

Pour this into the prepared tray and bake for 25–30 minutes until the top is crisp and the centre is slightly soft.

Leave to cool in the tin before slicing up. Serve the blondies with a dollop of whipped cream and a light dusting of cinnamon.

banana bread blondies

Makes 12

The classic flavours of banana bread but in fudgy blondie-bar form, topped with caramelized banana slices.

4 ripe bananas
200g (7oz) unsalted butter, melted
1 egg
250g (9oz) light brown sugar
1 tsp vanilla extract
170g (6oz) plain (all-purpose) flour
2 tsp ground cinnamon
½ tsp salt
½ tsp baking powder
2 tbsp caster (superfine) sugar,
   to sprinkle on top

Preheat the oven to 170°C fan (325°F/gas 5) and grease and line a 20 x 30cm (8 x 12in) baking tin with greaseproof paper.

Mash up two of the ripe bananas in a large bowl, then add the melted butter, egg, light brown sugar and vanilla and whisk together.

In a separate bowl, whisk together the flour, cinnamon, salt and baking powder, then fold this into the wet mixture until just combined. Pour the batter into the prepared tin and gently smooth it level.

Slice up the remaining bananas into 5mm (¼in) slices on the diagonal and lay these over the surface of the blondie. Sprinkle the caster sugar evenly over the top and bake for 25–30 minutes until the bananas are caramelized with a crisp sugar crust and if you insert a knife into the blondie beneath, it comes out semi-clean.

Leave to cool in the tin completely before slicing up.

plum crumble blondies

Makes 9–16

Soft and tart roasted plums are baked into a fudgy blondie topped with spiced crumble. If you're not a star anise fan, you can swap it out for cinnamon or ground ginger – both are equally delicious.

For the blondie base
200g (7oz) unsalted butter, melted
250g (9oz) light brown sugar
2 eggs
1 tsp vanilla extract
200g (7oz) plain (all-purpose) flour
½ tsp salt
½ tsp baking powder
5 large plums, stones removed,
    cut into quarters

For the crumble
70g (2½oz) plain (all-purpose) flour
Pinch of salt
30g (1oz) light brown sugar
½ tsp ground star anise
50g (1¾oz) butter, chilled and cubed

Preheat the oven to 170ºC fan (325ºF/gas 5) and grease and line a 23cm (9in) square baking tin with greaseproof paper.

First make the crumble topping. Put the flour, salt, sugar and ground star anise in a bowl, then rub in the butter until you have coarse crumbs. Squeeze small handfuls of the crumble to clump some of it together so that you have chunky crumble pieces, then put in the fridge to chill until you're ready to use.

To make the blondie base, whisk together the melted butter, sugar, eggs and vanilla in a large bowl.

In a separate bowl, whisk together the flour, salt and baking powder, then fold this into the wet mixture.

Pour the blondie batter into the prepared tray, and scatter over the plum quarters, pushing some down into the blondie and making sure they're evenly distributed. Scatter the crumble over the top and bake for 30–35 minutes until an inserted knife comes out clean and the crumble topping is golden brown.

Leave to cool in the tin completely before slicing up.

buckwheat and peanut butter blondies

gf

Makes 12

Buckwheat flour is made from a flowering plant. It's more nutrient-rich than plain wheat flour and, despite its name, it doesn't contain wheat and is therefore gluten free. It has a distinctive nutty flavour, so it's really good with peanut butter.

220g (7¾oz) unsalted butter
3 eggs
300g (10½oz) light brown sugar
1 tsp vanilla extract
160g (5¾oz) buckwheat flour
40g (1½oz) ground almonds
1 tsp flaky salt, plus extra for sprinkling on top
150g (5½oz) peanut butter (crunchy or
    smooth – your preference)
100g (3½oz) milk chocolate, broken into chunks

Preheat the oven to 160ºC fan (315ºF/gas 4) and grease and line a 20 x 30cm (8 x 12in) baking tin with greaseproof paper.

Make the brown butter by melting the butter gently in a small saucepan. Once melted, turn up the heat to medium and cook until the butter turns golden brown and you can see tiny specks of brown at the bottom of the pan, and it starts to smell nutty. This usually takes a few minutes; whisk occasionally so that it doesn't catch on the bottom of the pan and keep a close eye on it so that you don't burn it! Set aside to cool slightly.

Whisk together the eggs, sugar and vanilla until thick and fluffy – this is best done with an electric whisk or in a freestanding mixer, if you have one. Then slowly pour in the browned butter while whisking until combined. Carefully fold in the buckwheat flour, ground almonds and salt.

Pour the batter into the prepared tray and dollop over the peanut butter. With a pallet knife, roughly swirl the peanut butter into the batter. Scatter over the chocolate chunks and give it another rough smooth over. Sprinkle over a little flaky salt.

Bake for 35–40 minutes until the edges are crisp and golden brown and the centre has just set.

Leave to cool completely in the tin before slicing up.

cherry bakewell blondies

Makes 9–16

Ground almonds make these blondies even fudgier and, topped with lashings of cherry jam and lemony glacé icing drizzle, here you have your classic bakewell tart flavour.

2 eggs

250g (9oz) light brown sugar

1 tsp almond extract

200g (7oz) unsalted butter, melted

100g (3½oz) plain (all-purpose) flour

200g (7oz) ground almonds

½ tsp salt

200g (7oz) cherry jam (or any other kind you like – apricot or raspberry jams are really good here too)

30g (1oz) flaked almonds

2 heaped tbsp icing (confectioners') sugar

Juice of ½ lemon

Preheat the oven to 170ºC fan (325ºF/gas 5) and grease and line a 23cm (9in) square baking tin with greaseproof paper.

Whisk up the eggs, sugar and almond extract until pale and fluffy – this is best done with an electric whisk or in a freestanding mixer, if you have one. Then whisk in the melted butter.

In a separate bowl, combine the flour, ground almonds and salt, then fold this into the eggs and sugar until just mixed through.

Pour the batter into the prepared tin and spread evenly. Dollop the jam over the surface and, with a teaspoon, swirl the jam into the batter ever so slightly. Sprinkle over the flaked almonds and bake for 25–30 minutes until the edges are crisp and the centre is firm but ever so slightly gooey.

Let it cool completely in the tin before making the glaze. Mix the icing sugar with the lemon juice – you want it to be opaque but runny. With a teaspoon, drizzle the glaze in a pattern over the blondie. If you can, wait 10 minutes for the icing to set before slicing up and serving.

brown butter honey and chai blondies

Makes 12

Browned butter just takes things one step further with its deeply nutty and rich flavour. This blondie is indulgent and warming with its chai spices and honey.

250g (9oz) unsalted butter
100g (3½oz) honey
2 eggs
200g (7oz) light brown sugar
1 tsp vanilla extract
200g (7oz) plain (all-purpose) flour
1½ tsp ground cardamom
1 tsp ground cinnamon
¾ tsp ground ginger
¼ tsp ground nutmeg
¼ tsp black pepper
½ tsp salt

Preheat the oven to 160ºC fan (315ºF/gas 4) and grease and line a 23cm (9in) square baking tin with greaseproof paper.

Firstly, brown the butter. Put it in a saucepan and heat on a low temperature at first to melt it. Once melted, turn up the heat to medium and cook until the butter turns golden brown and you can see tiny specks of brown at the bottom of the pan, and it starts to smell nutty. This usually takes a few minutes; whisk occasionally so that it doesn't catch on the bottom of the pan and keep a close eye on it so that you don't burn it! Take the pan off the heat and stir in the honey until melted.

In a large bowl, whisk together the eggs, brown sugar and vanilla until frothy, then whisk in the brown butter honey.

In a separate bowl, whisk together the flour, spices and salt, then fold this carefully into the batter mixture.

Pour the batter into the prepared tin and bake for 25–30 minutes until the edges are crisp and the middle is still slightly gooey.

Leave to cool completely in the tin before slicing up.

matcha strawberry and blond chocolate blondies

Makes 9

Earthy matcha, caramelized blond chocolate, sweet but tart strawberries – this is a matcha made in heaven. I'm not sorry.

2 eggs

300g (10½oz) light brown sugar

1 tsp vanilla extract

250g (9oz) unsalted butter, melted

200g (7oz) plain (all-purpose) flour

½ tsp salt

2 tbsp matcha powder

150g (5½oz) blond chocolate, chopped into
large chunks

150g (5½oz) strawberries, hulled and sliced

Preheat the oven to 160°C fan (315°F/gas 4) and grease and line a 23cm (9in) square baking tin with greaseproof paper.

Whisk the eggs, sugar and vanilla together in a large bowl until frothy – this is best done with an electric whisk or in a freestanding mixer, if you have one. Then slowly whisk in the melted butter.

In a separate bowl, combine the flour, salt and matcha, then fold this carefully into the eggs and sugar, followed by the chocolate chunks.

Pour the batter into the prepared tin, smooth level with a pallet knife and scatter over the strawberry slices.

Bake for 30 minutes or until the edges are crisp and the middle is slightly gooey.

Leave to cool completely in the tin before slicing up.

pistachio knafeh blondies

Makes 9

You can buy kadayif pastry online, or in most Turkish supermarkets. It's a pastry made of tiny shredded wheat noodles, and when they're crisped up with a bit of butter and combined with creamy pistachio spread – my god, it's good.

For the blondie base
2 eggs
200g (7oz) light brown sugar
1 tsp vanilla extract
250g (9oz) unsalted butter, melted
200g (7oz) plain (all-purpose) flour
1 tsp salt

For the pistachio knafeh
30g (1oz) unsalted butter
100g (3½oz) kadayif pastry, roughly chopped
200g (7oz) pistachio cream
100g (3½oz) dark chocolate, melted
50g (1¾oz) chopped or slivered pistachios

Preheat the oven to 150ºC fan (300ºF/gas 3) and grease and line a 23cm (9in) square baking tin with greaseproof paper.

Whisk the eggs, sugar and vanilla together until frothy – this is best done with an electric whisk or in a freestanding mixer, if you have one. Then slowly whisk in the melted butter. Carefully fold in the flour and salt until just combined, then pour the batter into the prepared tin and smooth level.

For the knafeh, melt the butter in a large frying pan, then add the kadayif pastry. Toast on a low–medium heat until the strands of pastry are golden brown, then take off the heat. Stir in the pistachio cream – it should melt and soften slightly in the warm pan – until combined.

Spoon chunks of this mixture on top of the blondie and ever so slightly smooth over. Bake for 25–30 minutes until the knafeh is a little golden on top and the blondie is still slightly soft in the middle.

Leave to cool completely in the tin before drizzling over the melted dark chocolate in a pattern, then scatter over the pistachios. Pop in the fridge for an hour or more before slicing up and serving.

crème brulée blondies

Makes 9–16

Crème brulée in blondie-bar form: smooth creamy custard with that butterscotch crackle on top – delectable.

For the blondie base

125g (4½oz) butter, melted
150g (5½oz) light brown sugar
1 egg
½ tsp vanilla extract
120g (4¼oz) plain (all-purpose) flour
Pinch of salt
¼ tsp baking powder

For the custard topping

1 vanilla pod
900g (2lb) double (heavy) cream
200ml (7fl oz) whole milk
10 egg yolks
120g (4¼oz) caster (superfine) sugar,
   plus extra for bruléeing
2 tbsp cornflour (cornstarch)
Pinch of salt

First make the blondie base. Preheat the oven to 160ºC fan (315ºF/gas 4) and grease and line a 23cm (9in) square baking tin with greaseproof paper.

In a large bowl, whisk together the melted butter, sugar, egg and vanilla extract until combined – this is best done with an electric whisk or in a freestanding mixer, if you have one.

In a separate bowl, whisk together the flour, salt and baking powder, then fold this into the wet mixture.

Pour the batter into the tin and ensure it's evenly spread. Bake for 15–20 minutes until a knife is inserted and it comes out with only a few moist crumbs. Leave to cool while you get on with the custard.

Cut the vanilla pod in half lengthways and with a small knife, scrape the vanilla seeds out. Add the seeds and the pod halves to a medium-sized saucepan, along with the double cream and milk and heat gently on low until it just starts to simmer, then turn off the heat.

In a large heatproof bowl, whip the egg yolks, caster sugar, cornflour and salt until pale and fluffy – this is easier with an electric whisk.

Temper the eggs by slowly adding the hot cream to the bowl a little at a time, while whisking to prevent the eggs from cooking, before adding the rest and whisking together. Pour this back into the pan and then, on a low–medium heat, stir until it thickens and becomes a creamy custard. Take off the heat and sieve it into a jug, discarding the vanilla pod. Pour the custard over the cooled blondie base and pop into the fridge for at least 4 hours, or overnight, to set.

When ready to serve, take the blondie out of the tin and slice it into squares, then scatter over the extra caster sugar. Using either a blowtorch or grill (broiler) on medium–high heat, brulée the sugar until golden brown and caramelized.

ext
ext
ext
ext

ras

ras

ras

ras

use up leftover brownies & blondies

In the highly unlikely event that you have any leftover brownies and blondies, here are some ideas for simple and delicious ways to recycle and use them up.

brownie s'mores

Top your brownie with some shop-bought marshmallows or Marshmallow Fluff. Toast lightly with a blowtorch, if you have one, or under a grill (broiler) on a medium heat for a few minutes until nicely charred and the marshmallow has started softening. Top with crumbled digestive biscuits or graham crackers.

brownie or blondie trifle

Break up your brownies or blondies into chunks and add to a dish or individual bowls/glasses. Drizzle over shop-bought chocolate or caramel sauce and pour over custard if you fancy it! Top with freshly whipped cream and whatever sprinkles or other edible decorations you like.

brownie or blondie crumble ice-cream topper

Crumble up leftover brownies or blondies and sprinkle over your favourite ice cream.

brownie or blondie cheesecake base

Using your favourite cheesecake recipe as a guide, swap the biscuits/crackers for brownies or blondies (using the same weight); blitz them up and press down into the lined cheesecake tin. Bake at 160ºC (315ºF), gas 4, for 15 minutes to dry out and firm up. Leave to cool, then top with the cheesecake filling. You can stir in more broken-up brownies and blondies into the cheesecake filling if you want an even more indulgent cheesecake!

brownie or blondie cookies

Chop up your brownies or blondies and add them to your favourite cookie-dough recipe before baking.

brownie or blondie ice-cream sandwich

Slice your brownie or blondie in half horizontally, if it's an extra chunky one, or take two if you want! Sandwich together with a scoop of your favourite ice cream.

fun index

Here are my personal favourite brownie
and blondie recipes for every occasion:

best to impress
Chocolate Mousse Brownies (see page 64)

best in summer
Malted Milk Brownie Ice Cream Sando
(see page 57)

best in winter
Skillet Chocolate Chestnut Brownie Pudding
(see page 52)

best vegan
Apple and Cinnamon Swirl Blondies
(see page 83)

best gluten-free
Flourless Almond and Sour Cherry Brownies
(see page 25)

best flavour
Matcha Strawberry and Blond Chocolate
Blondies (see page 129)

best gooey
Triple Choc Brownies (see page 16)

brand/suppliers list

These are the brands I like to use for
my brownies:

chocolate
Guittard, Lindt, Green and Black's

flour
Doves Farm

sugar
Tate & Lyle

butter
Lurpak

vegan butter
Flora Plant Butter

salt
Maldon

vanilla extract or vanilla bean paste
Taylor & Colledge

online retailers

uk
www.ocado.com – essential baking ingredients
www.bakkalim.co.uk/groceries – kadayif, halva,
   slivered pistachios, rose water etc.
www.longdan.co.uk – pandan extract
www.souschef.co.uk – speciality ingredients

australia
www.wholefoodsmerchants.com
www.essentialingredient.com.au
www.fooddistribute.com.au

us
www.traderjoes.com/home

brownies around the world

Some great bakeries in the UK, US, Europe and
Australia that sell delicious brownies and blondies:

uk
Pudding Stop – St Albans
Violet Bakery – London

australia
The Brownie Bar – Melbourne
Luxe Bakery – Sydney

us
The Fat Witch Bakery – New York
The Baked Bear – San Francisco
Based in Brooklyn – New York

france
Angelina – Paris
Stoney Clove Bakery – Paris

germany
Nano Kaffee – Berlin
Cupcake Berlin – Berlin

belgium
Quetzal – Antwerp
Renard Bakery – Ixelles

austria
Baltram – Feine Patisserie – Salzburg
Demel – Vienna

index

about the author

As well as a cookbook author and recipe developer, I am a self-taught food stylist for cookbooks, commercial stills, films and TV. I started my career in food at The Hummingbird Bakery, where I learned the basics of cupcakes, cake decorating and classic bakes. I then moved to Claire Ptak's Violet Cakes, where I was head baker for over four years. Here I learned about seasonal fresh ingredients and a love of creativity and aesthetics further enhanced by an internship at Chez Panisse in Berkeley California, famed for Alice Waters' farm-to-table movement. Since then, I've worked with numerous publications and brands, such as Quadrille, Octopus, The White Company and *GQ*. Alongside, I've also worked on various films and TV shows, such as *Cruella*, *The Favourite*, *The Crown* and *Beetlejuice 2*, where my baking skills have been put to good use – creating anything from an 18th-century banquet to an 8-foot cake that has to fall to the ground or have a man thrown into it. I definitely prefer making delicious cakes and bakes for people to eat.

acknowledgements

Thank you so much to the Quadrille team: Stacey Cleworth for commissioning me to make this delicious book and Issy Gonzalez-Prendergast for taking over and bearing with my slow replies. And thank you to Katy Everett for designing it and making it look gorgeous.

To the shoot team, Matt and Federica for being able to make each shot of brown squares look different and unique, (and for cracking out the chrome toaster for some epic lighting). To Max for getting beautiful props to elevate the brown squares. And to Lu and Bea for helping me bake countless brownies and blondies. Gus (my dog) for eating the crumbs off the floor.

To my wonderful friend Kim who helped me test the recipes and gave me the most detailed feedback ever, and my amazing partner Jahn for heroically taste testing each recipe even though he's adamant he doesn't have a sweet tooth.

And last but not least to my little boy Nuri, who I was pregnant with during the writing and shooting of this book. He is my best bake to date.